THE VERY BEST OF
DIANA
KRALL

Photography: JAMES O'MARA

Alfred Music
P.O. Box 10003
Van Nuys, CA 91410-0003
alfred.com

CONTENTS

'S WONDERFUL

Music and Lyrics by
GEORGE GERSHWIN and IRA GERSHWIN

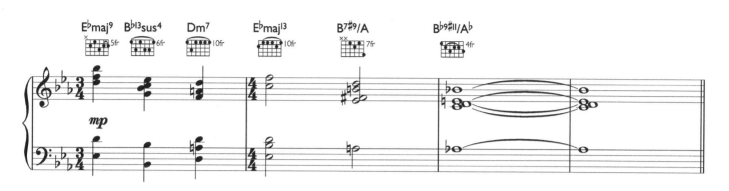

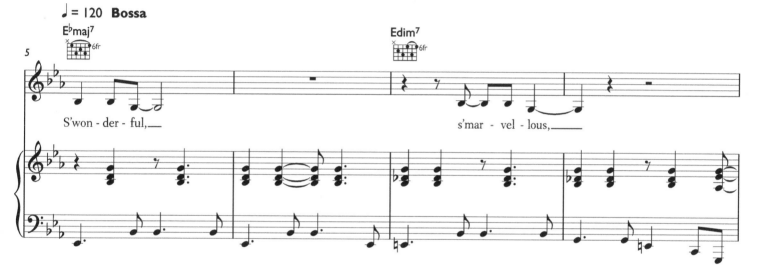

S'won-der-ful,___ s'mar - vel - lous,___

you___ should care___ for___ me.

'S Wonderful - 9 - 1

4

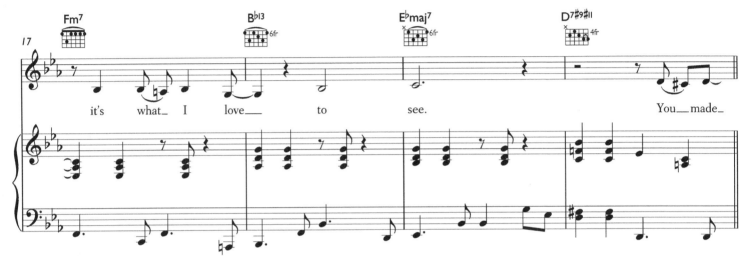

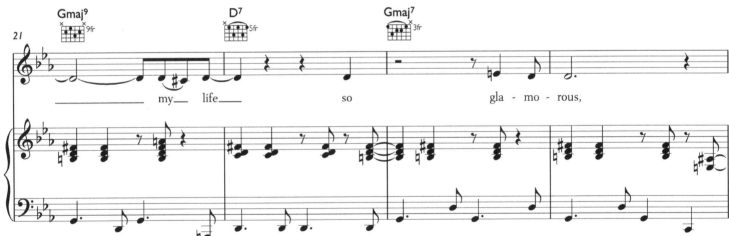

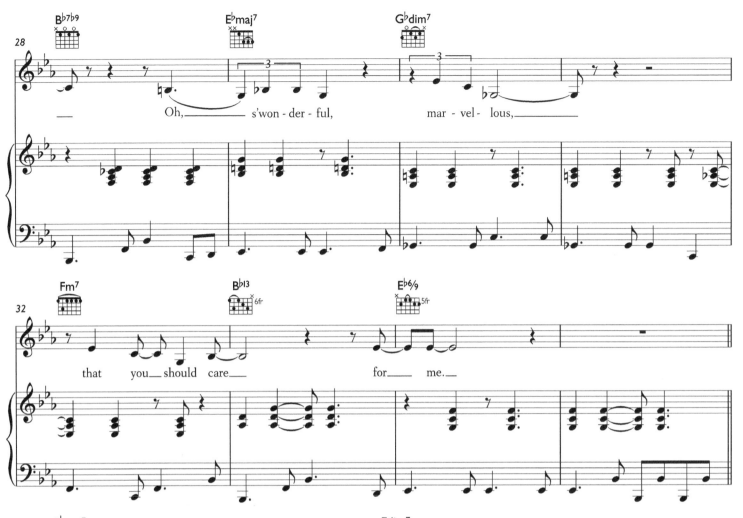

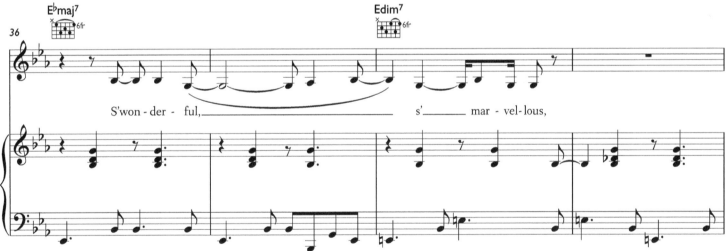

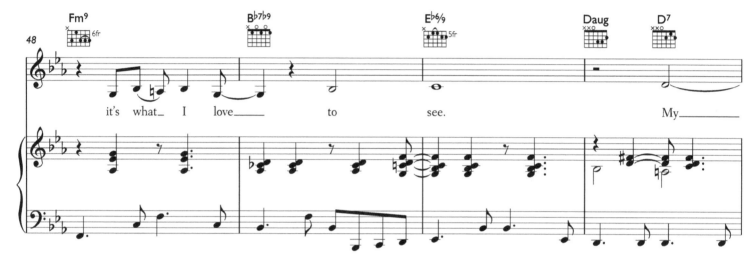

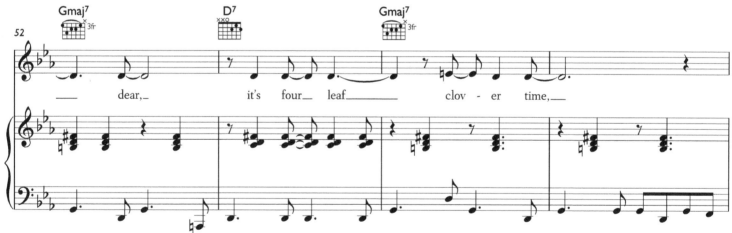

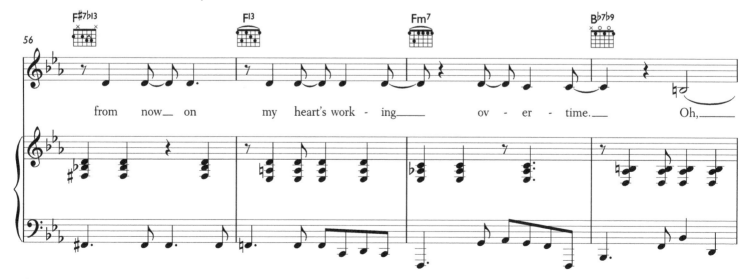

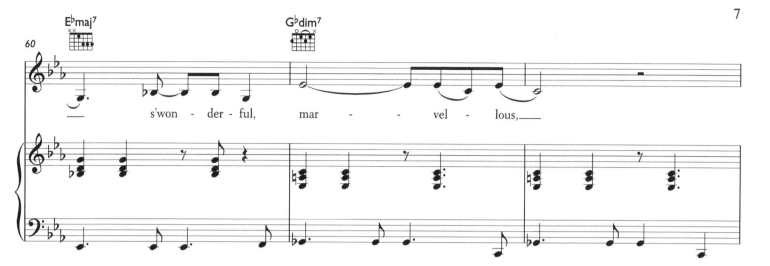

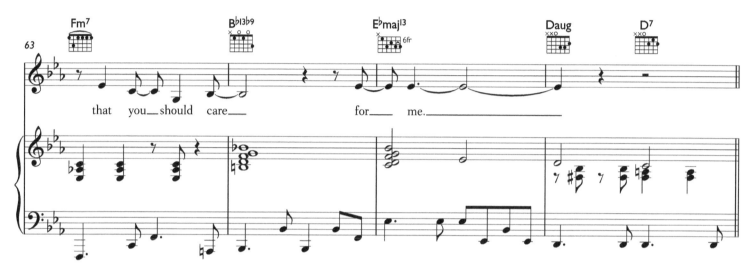

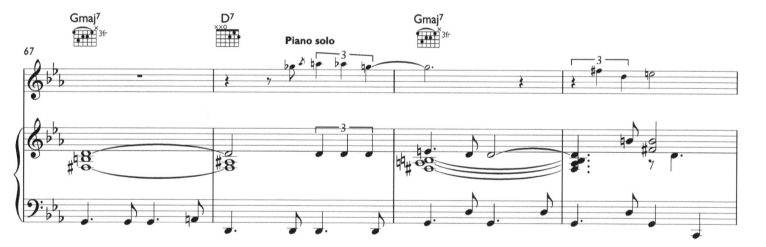

8

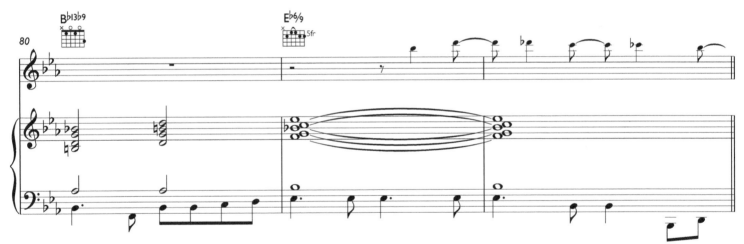

S'won - der - ful,_____ it's mar - vel - lous,_____

you—should care—— for me.

It's aw-f'lly nice,—— it's Pa - ra - dise,—

it's what— I love—— to see. You——

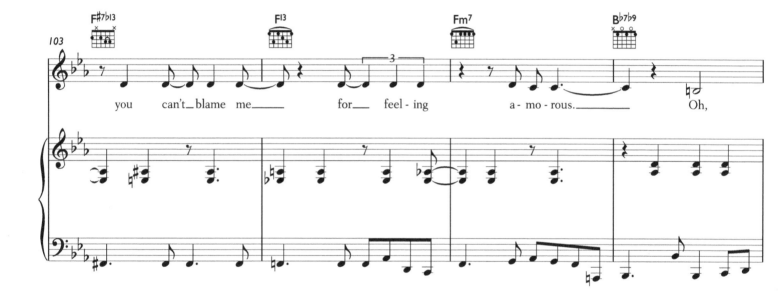

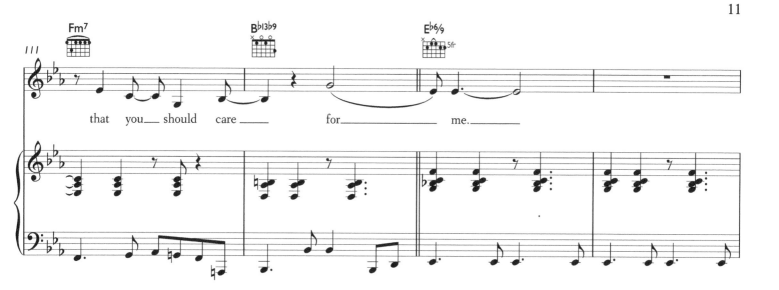

that you___ should care _____ for_____ me._____

PEEL ME A GRAPE

Words and Music by
DAVE FRISHBERG

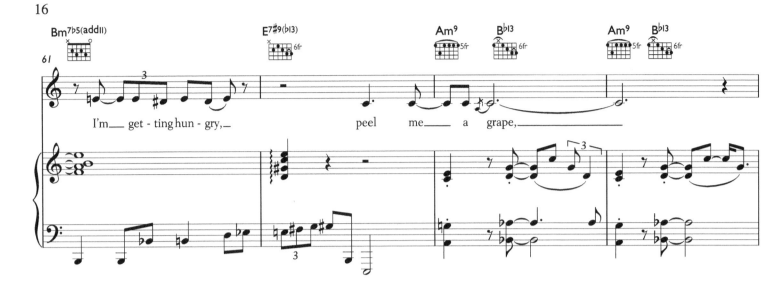

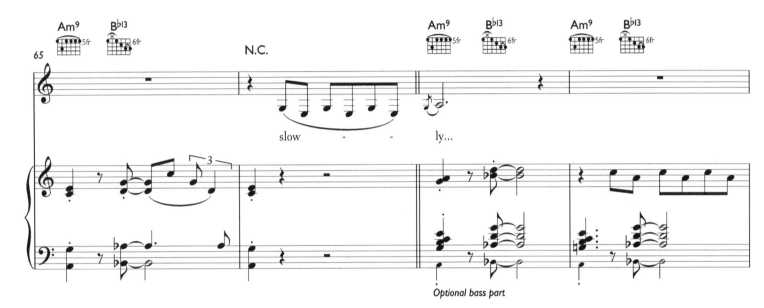

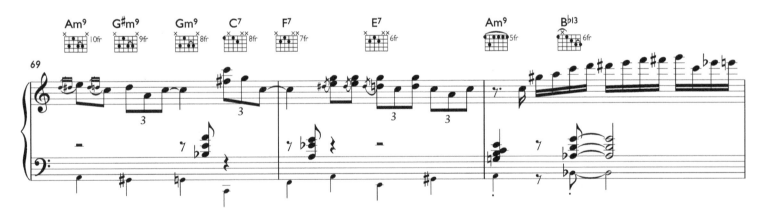

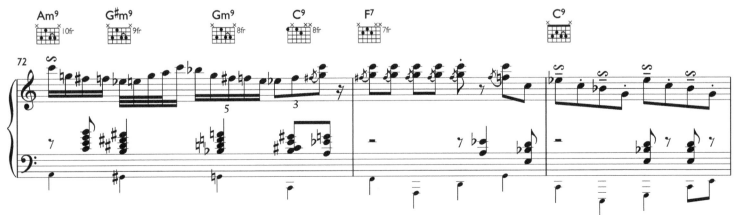

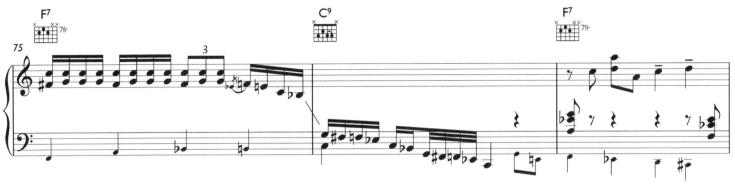

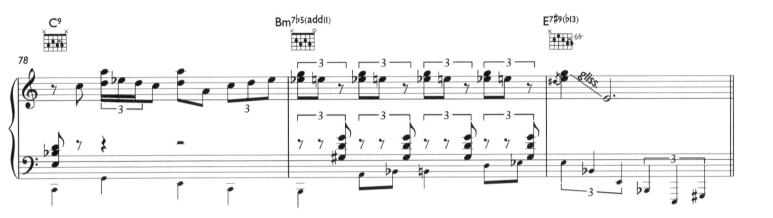

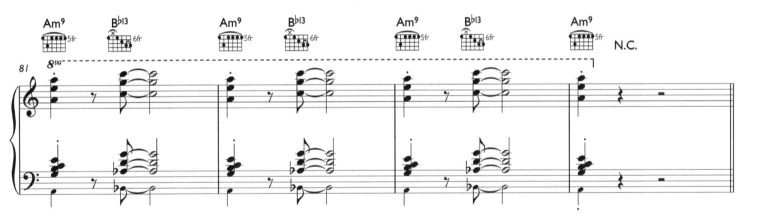

Here's how to be an ag-ree-ab-le chap,— love me and leave me in lux-u-ry's lap,— hop—

19

Peel Me a Grape - 9 - 8

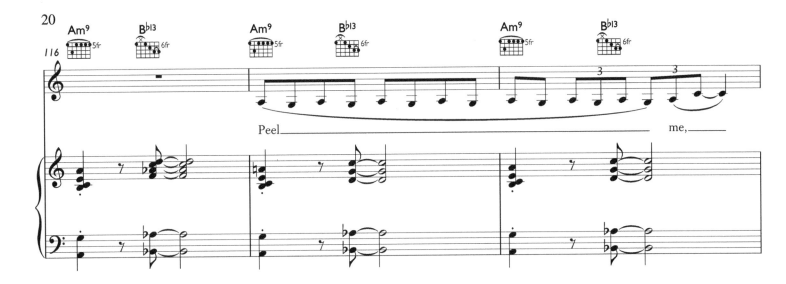

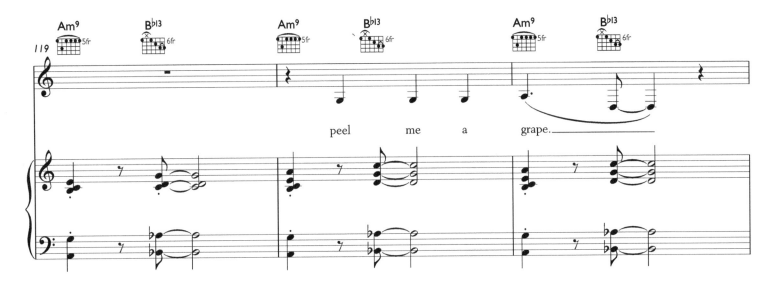

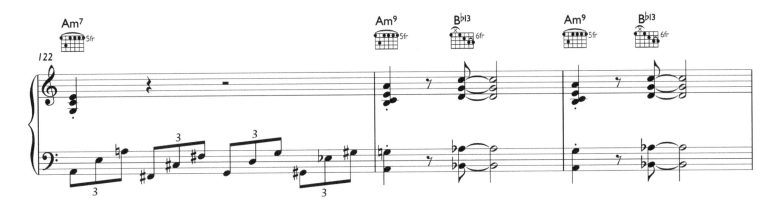

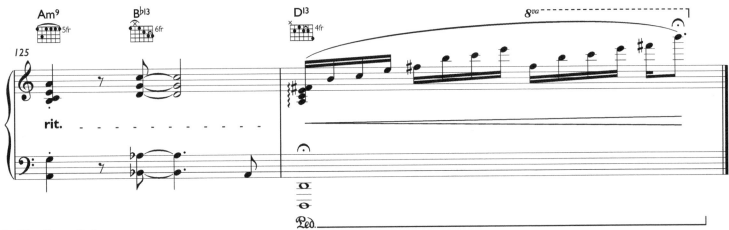

PICK YOURSELF UP

Words by
DOROTHY FIELDS

Music by
JEROME KERN

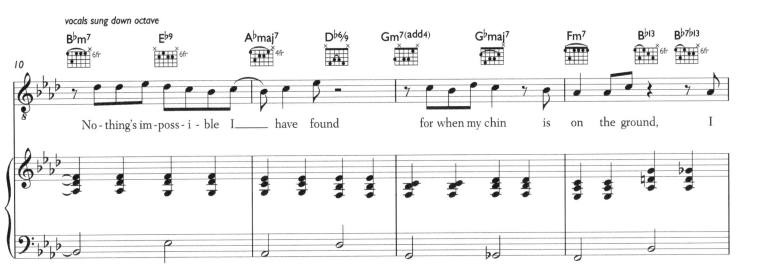

No - thing's im - poss - i - ble I____ have found for when my chin is on the ground, I

Pick Yourself Up - 5 - 1

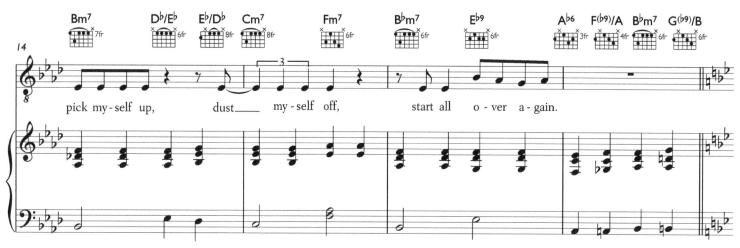

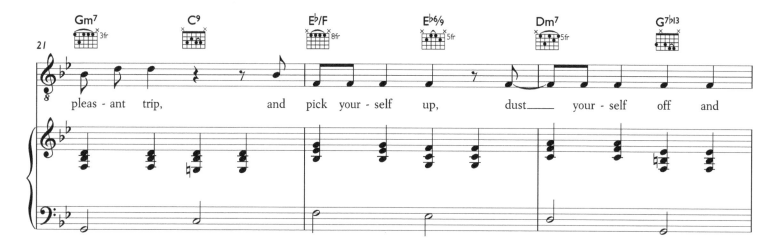

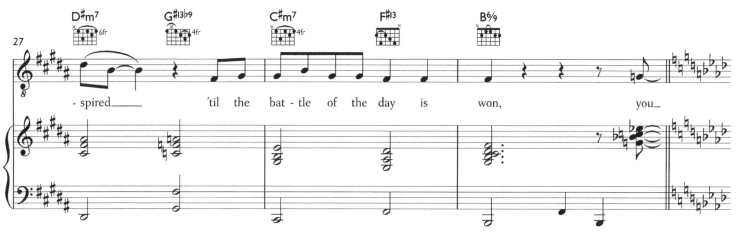

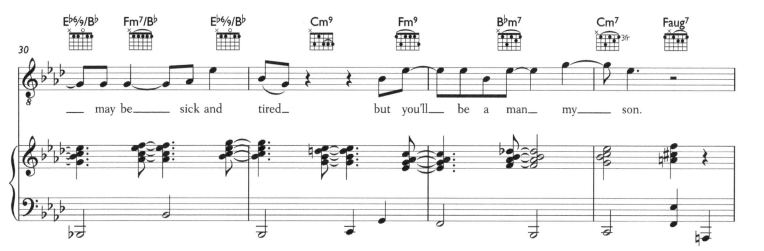

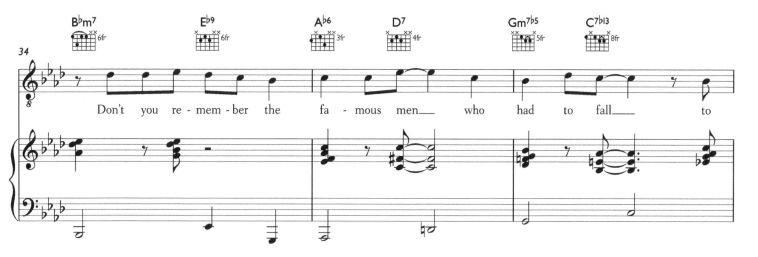

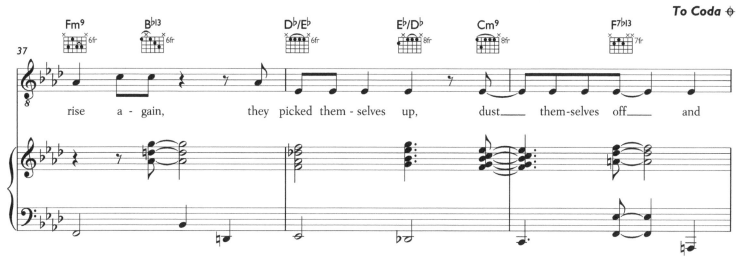

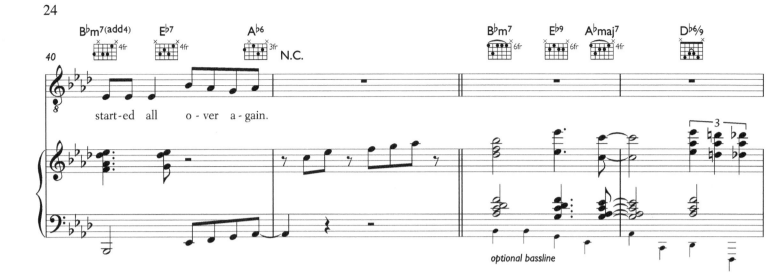

start-ed all o - ver a - gain.

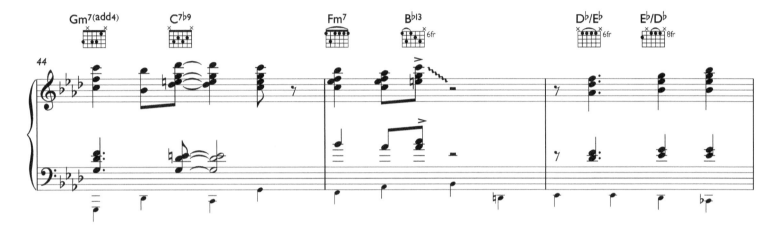

optional bassline

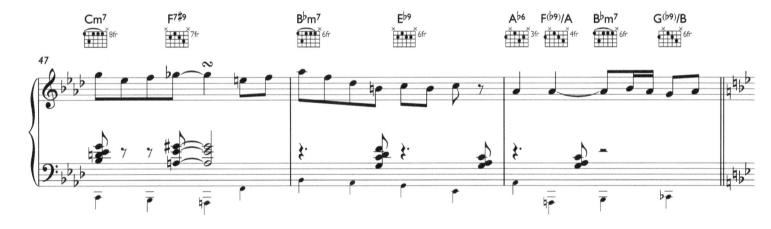

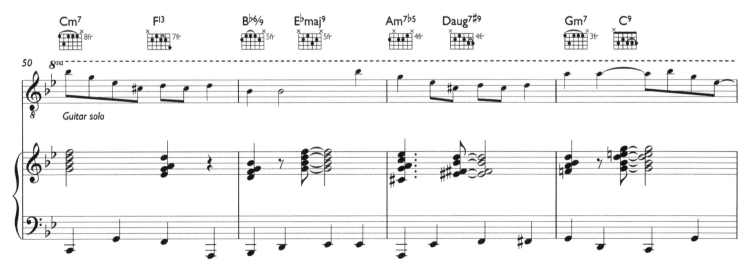

Guitar solo

⊕ Coda

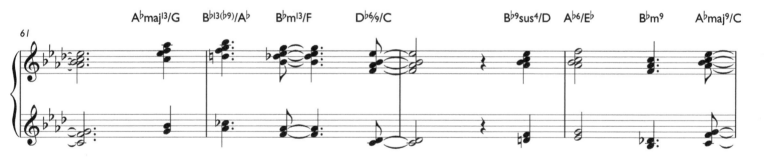

start - ed all o - ver a - gain.

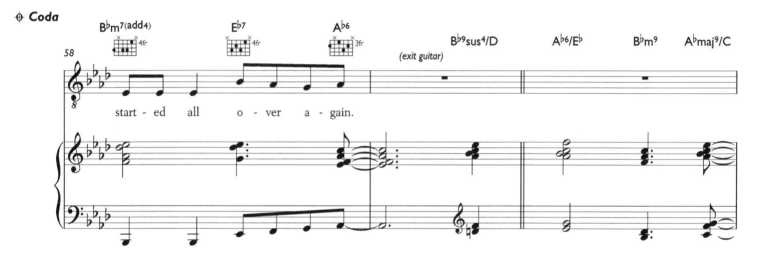

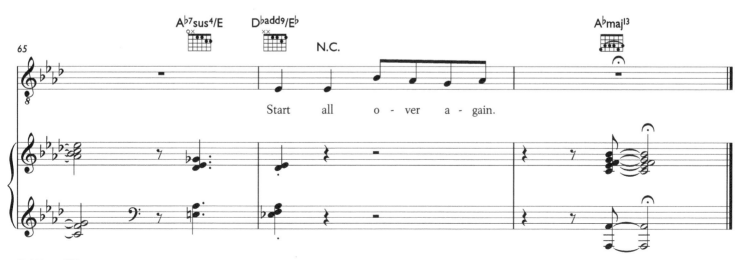

Start all o - ver a - gain.

YOU GO TO MY HEAD

Words by
HAVEN GILLESPIE

Music by
J. FRED COOTS

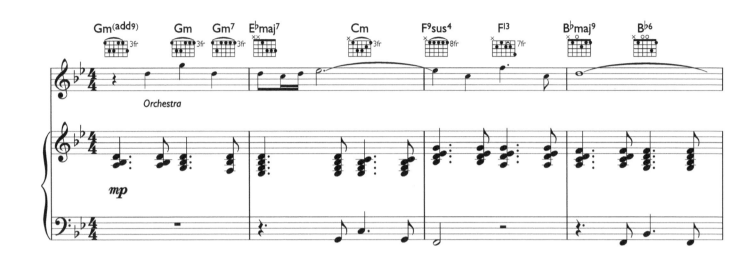

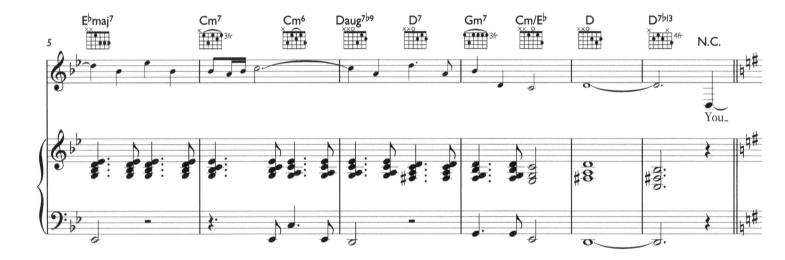

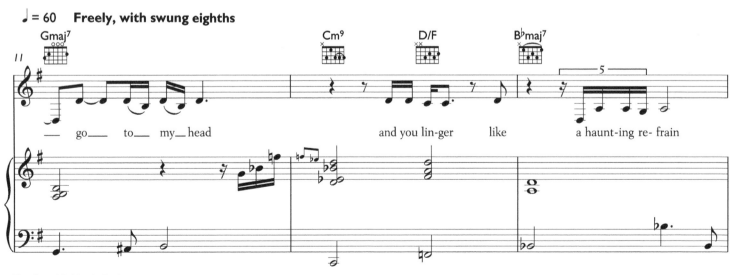

You Go to My Head - 6 - 1

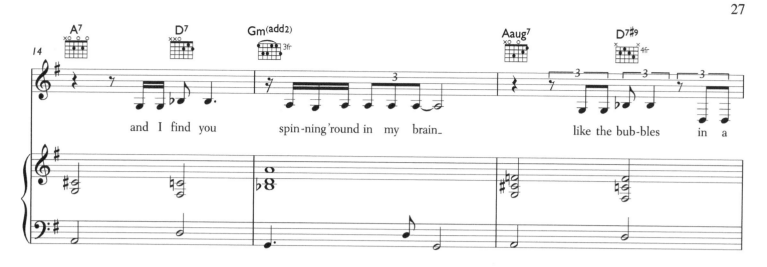

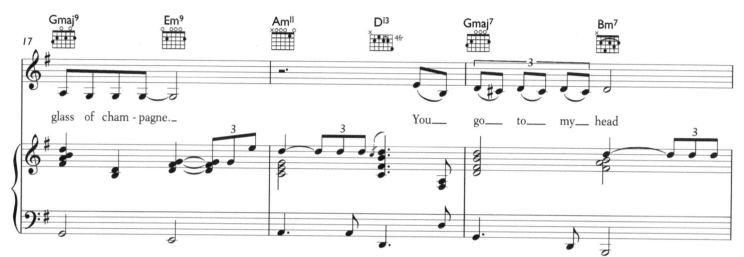

28

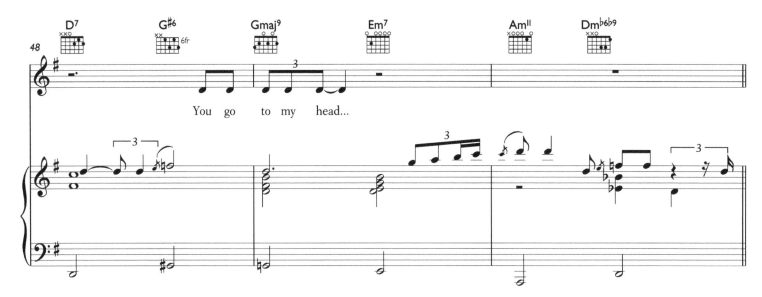

You go to my head...

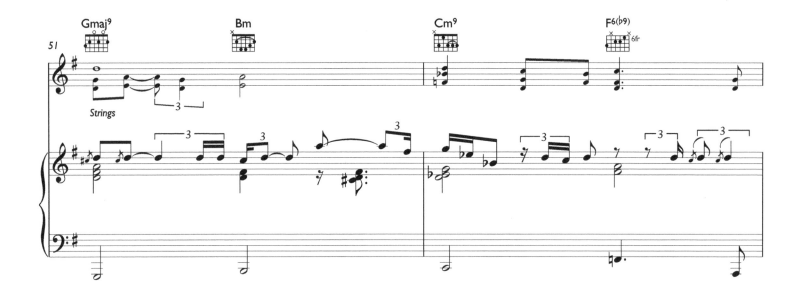

Strings

D.%. al Coda

⊕ *Coda*

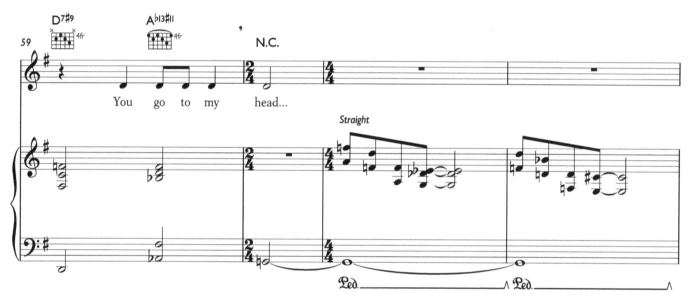

You go to my head...

FRIM FRAM SAUCE

Words and Music by
JOE RICARDEL and REDD EVANS

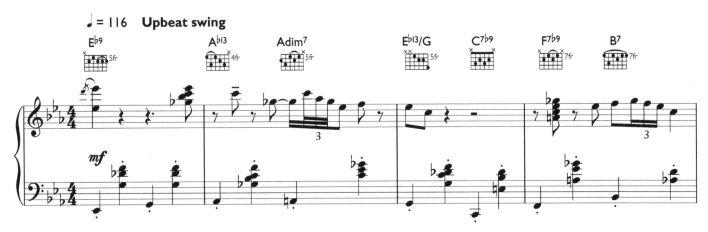

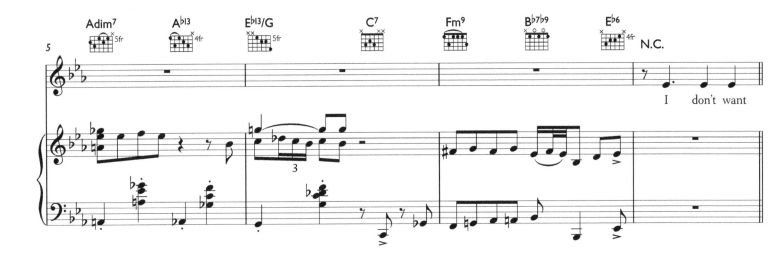

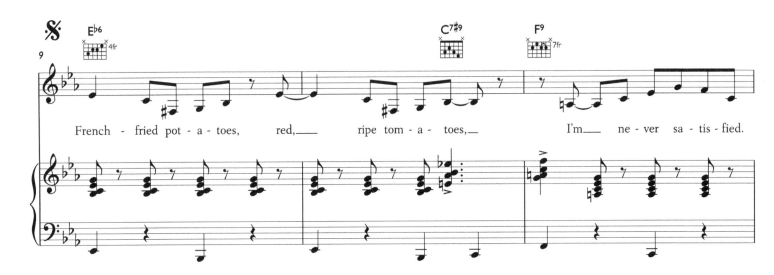

Frim Fram Sauce - 7 - 4

36

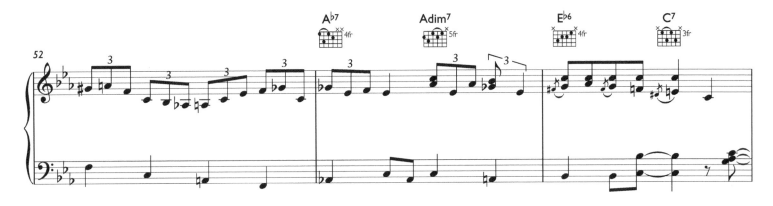

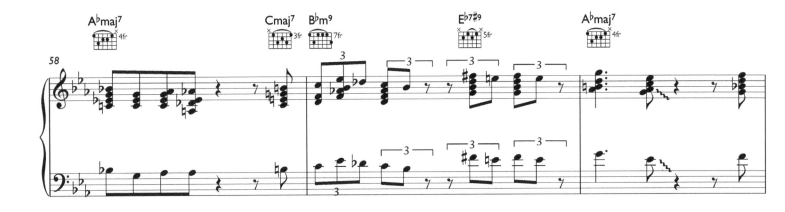

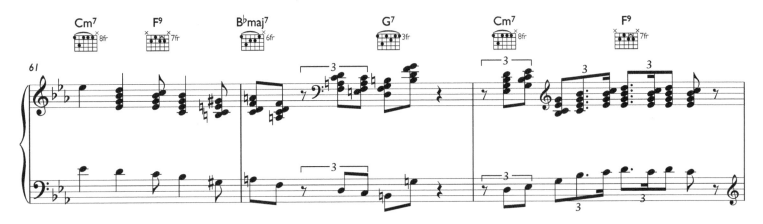

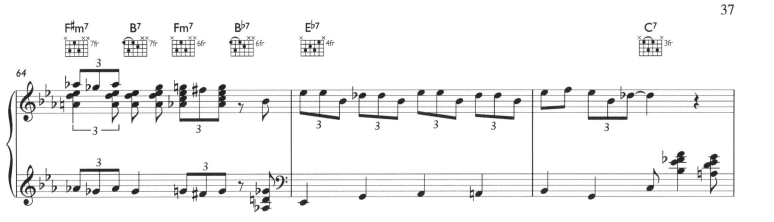

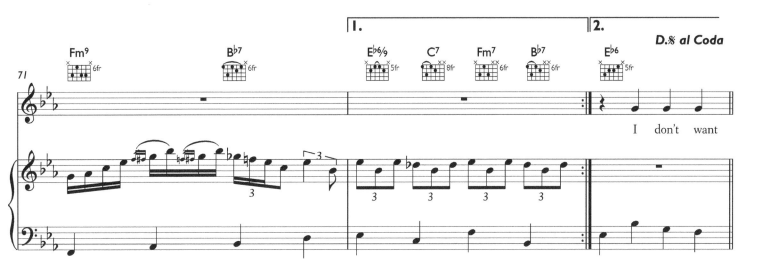

I don't want

38

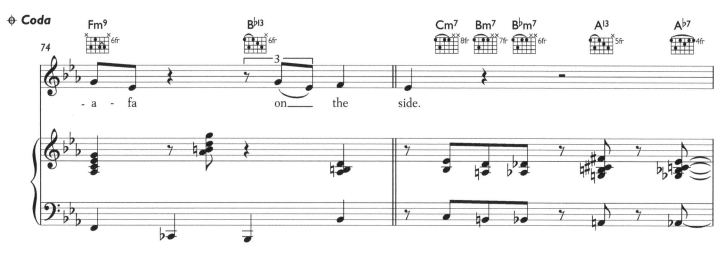

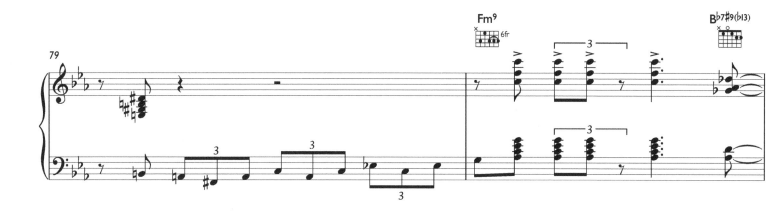

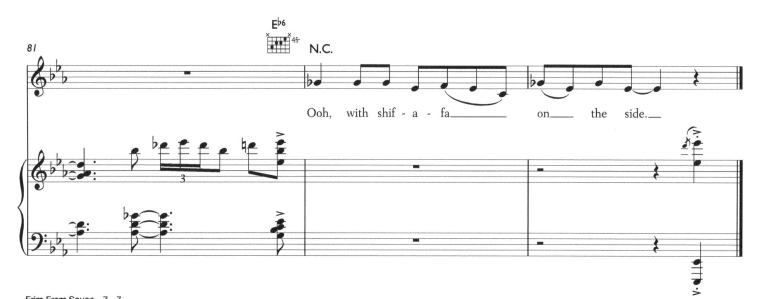

LET'S FALL IN LOVE

Words by
TED KOEHLER

Music by
HAROLD ARLEN

Let's Fall in Love - 7 - 1

40

42

Let's fall in love,___ why should-n't we fall in love?___ Now___ is the

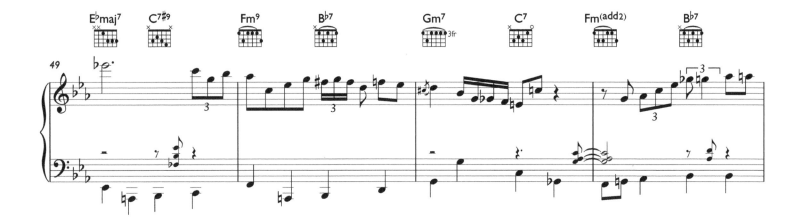

time for it, while we are young, let's__ fall in love.__

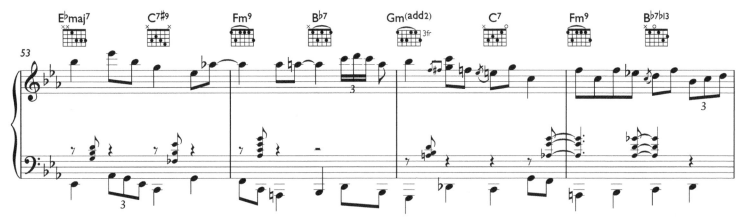

Let's Fall in Love - 7 - 4

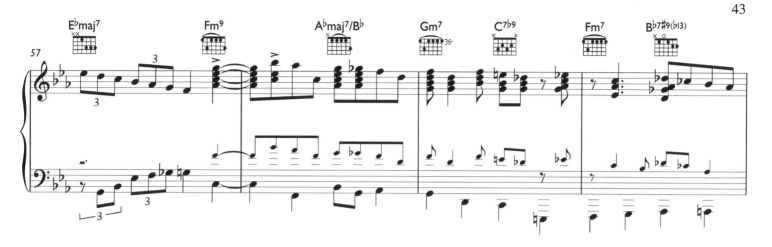

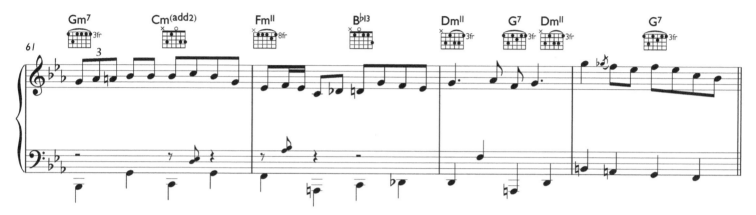

Let's Fall in Love - 7 - 5

44

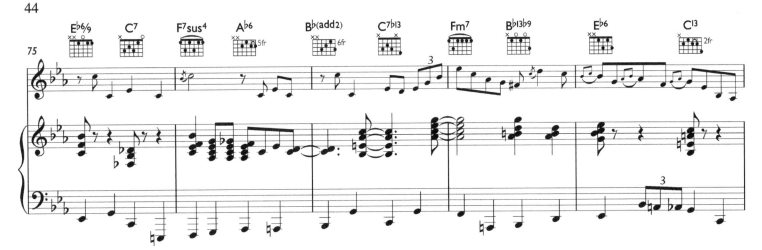

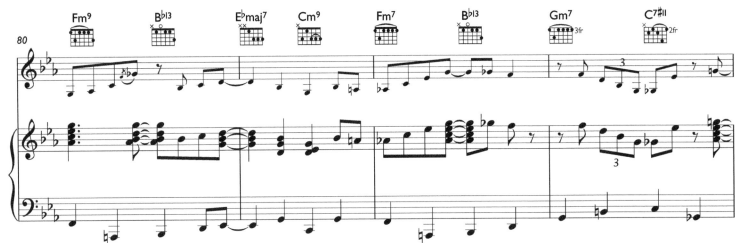

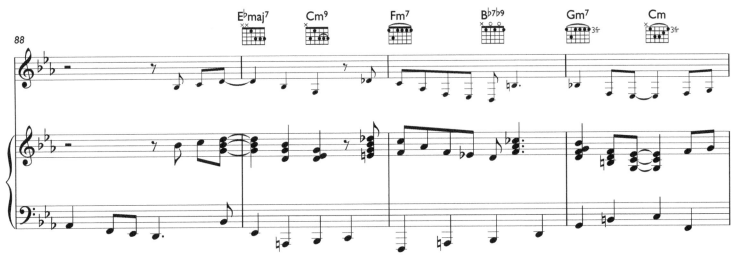

THE LOOK OF LOVE

Words by
HAL DAVID

Music by
BURT BACHARACH

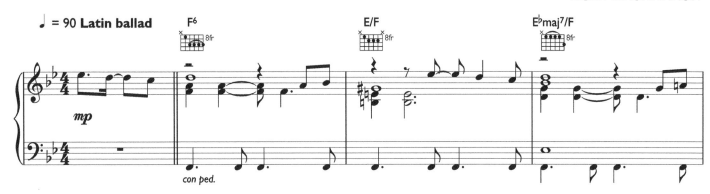

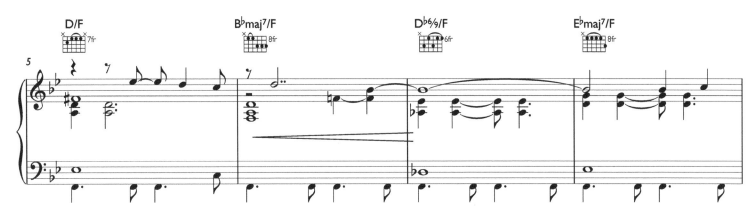

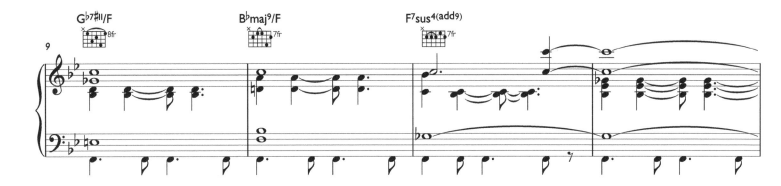

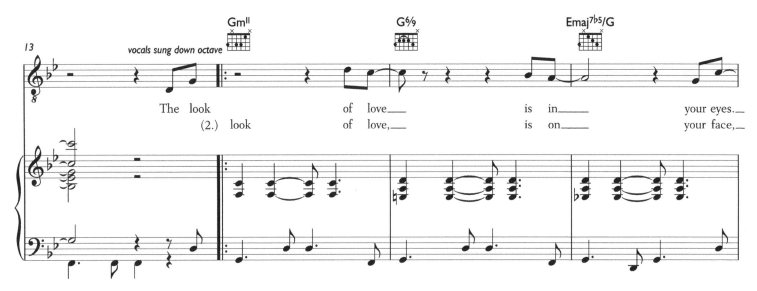

The look of love___ is in___ your eyes.
(2.) look of love,___ is on___ your face,

The Look of Love - 6 - 2

48

E♭maj7/F
F13♭9
Gm11
-er go,
I love you
so.
G6/9
Emaj7♭5/G
G6/9
B♭maj13
C6/D
A♭9/D
Gm9
Gm11
B♭7♭9♯11
E♭maj7
A♭13/E♭
B♭maj7

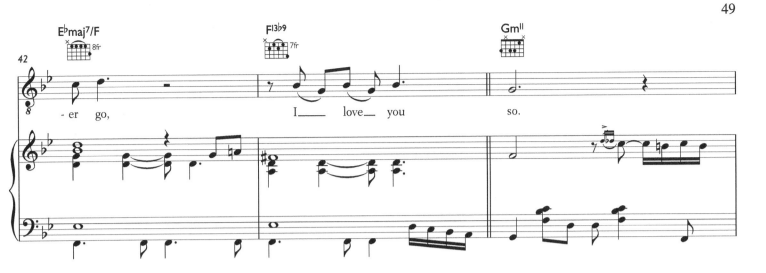

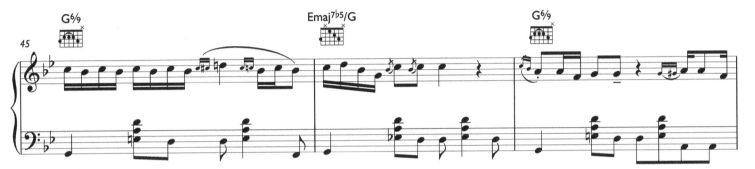

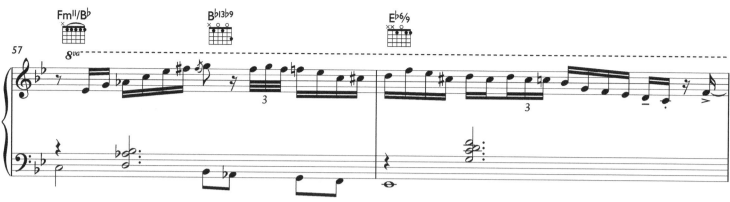

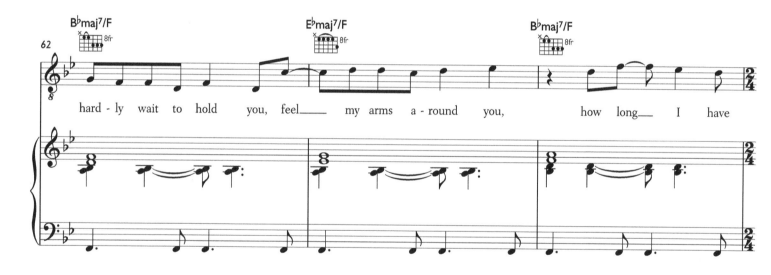

EAST OF THE SUN
(AND WEST OF THE MOON)

Words and Music by
BROOKS BOWMAN

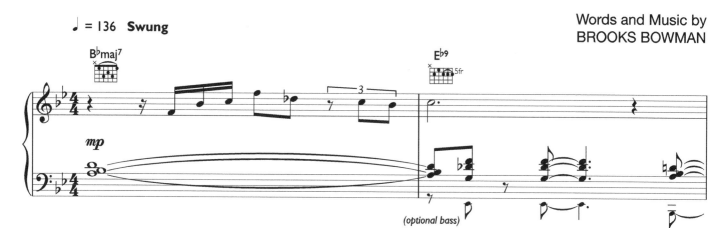

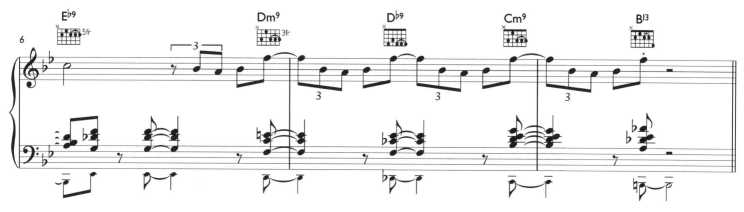

East of the Sun (and West of the Moon) - 4 - 1

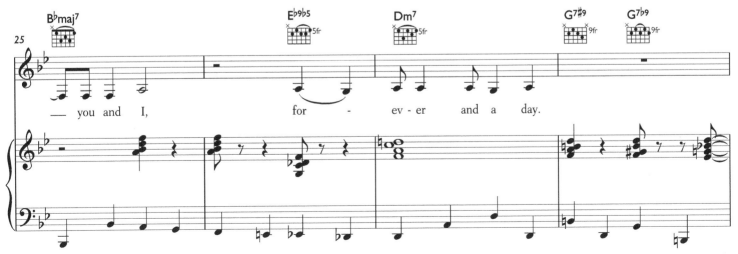

East of the Sun (and West of the Moon) - 4 - 2

Love will not die,____ we'll____ keep___ it that way.

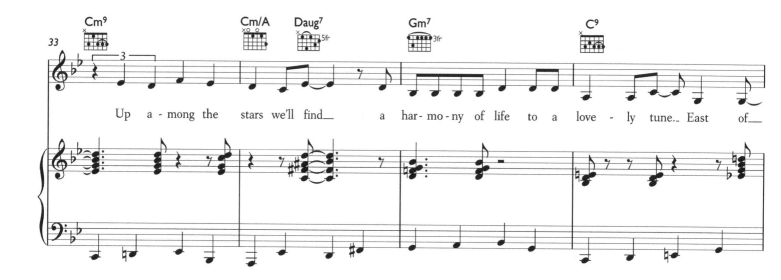

Up a - mong the stars we'll find___ a har - mo - ny of life to a love - ly tune._ East of__

__ the sun,__ west_ of the moon,___ dear.___ East

54

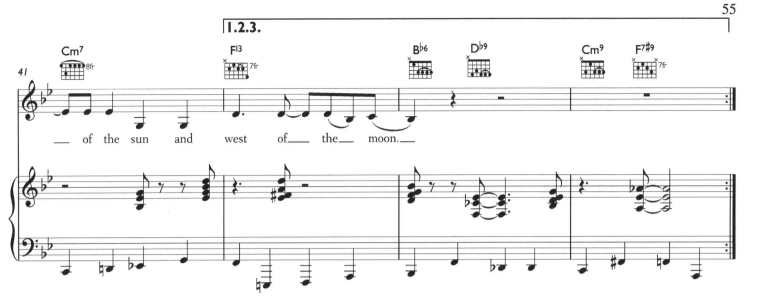

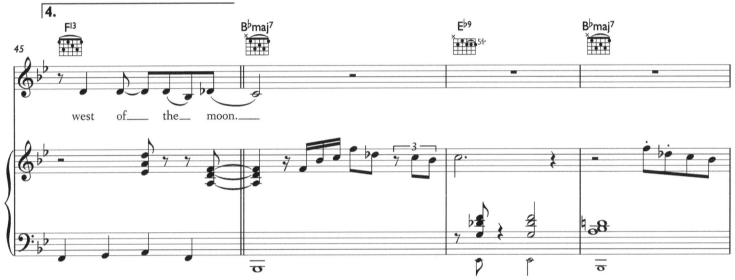

(Optional bass)

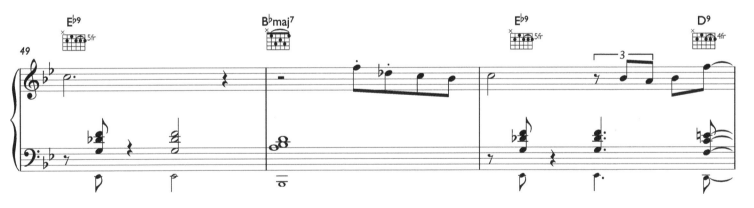

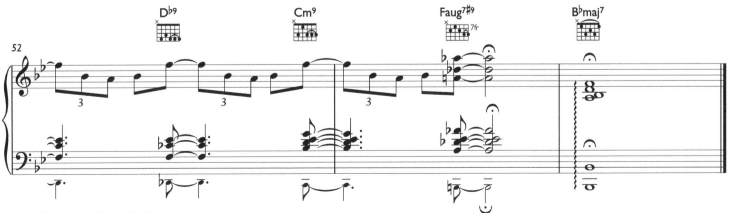

East of the Sun (and West of the Moon) - 4 - 4

I'VE GOT YOU UNDER MY SKIN

Words and Music by
COLE PORTER

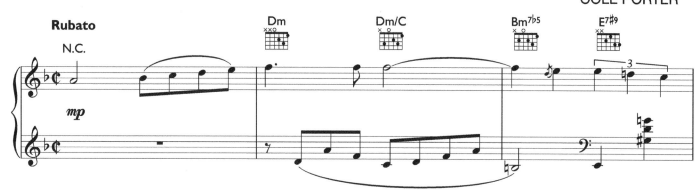

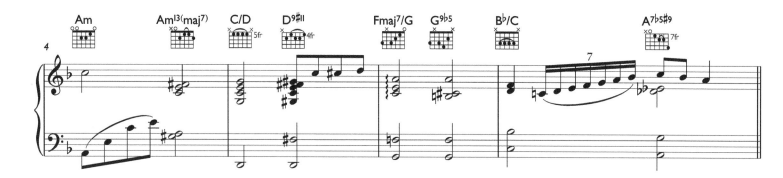

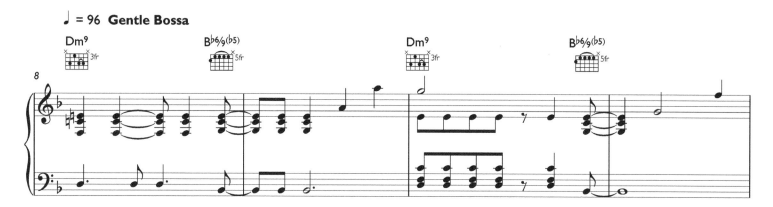

(vocals down octave)

I've

I've Got You Under My Skin - 7 - 1

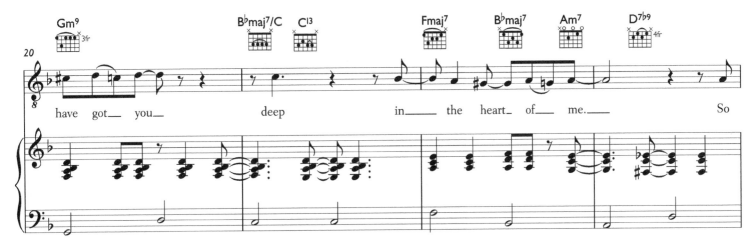

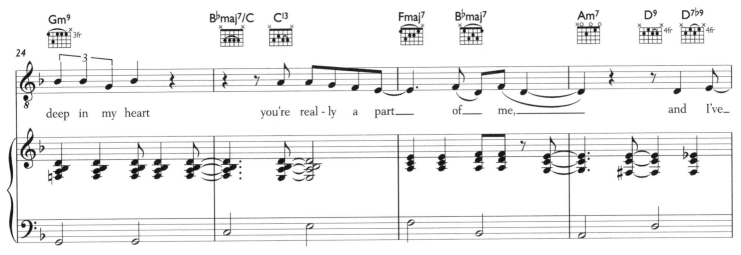

58

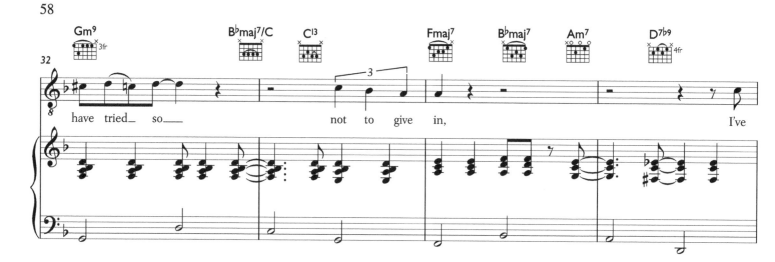

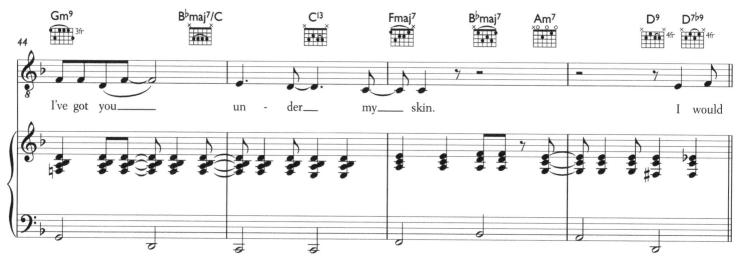

_ I_ do, just the thought of you_ makes me stop be-fore I be - gin, be-cause I've

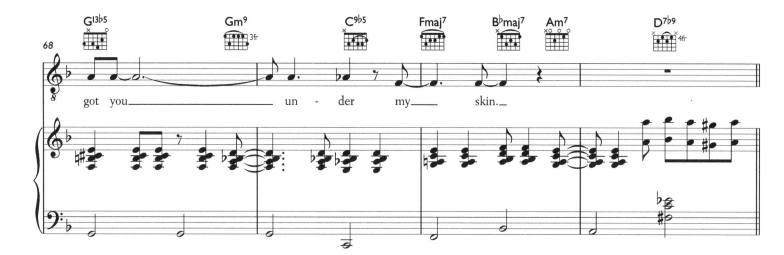

got you_____ un - der my___ skin._

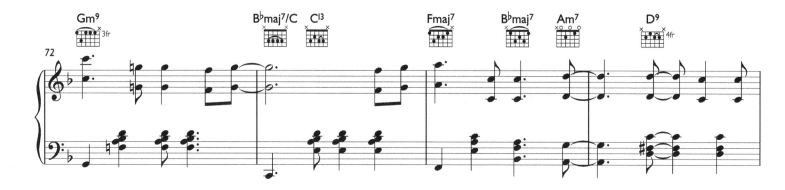

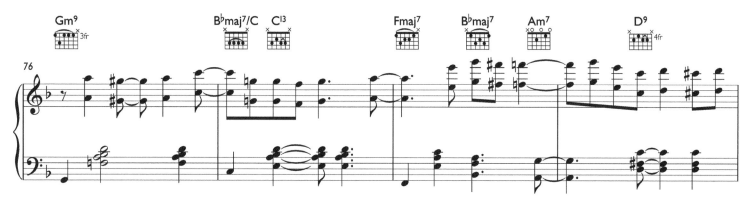

D.% al Coda

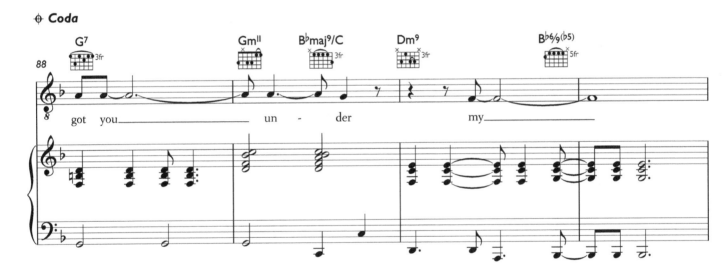

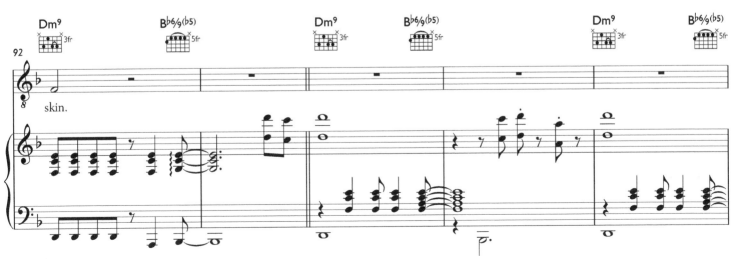

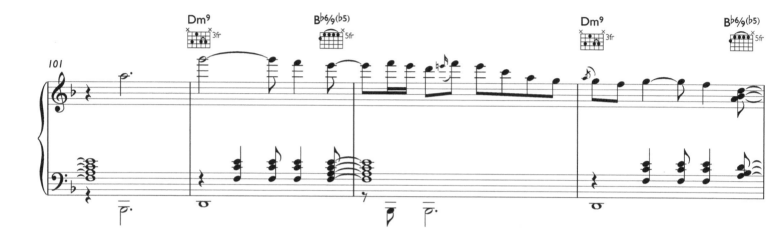

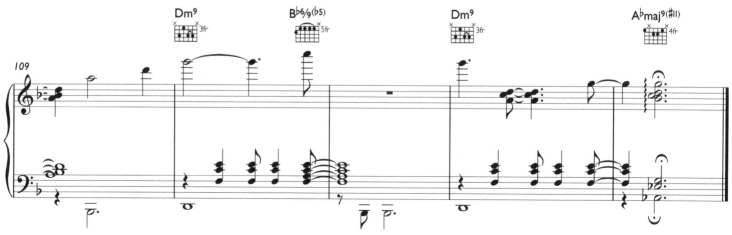

LET'S FACE THE MUSIC AND DANCE

Words and Music by
IRVING BERLIN

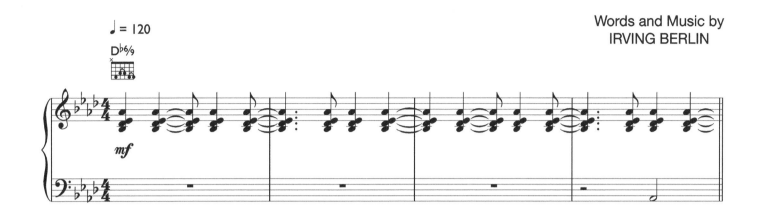

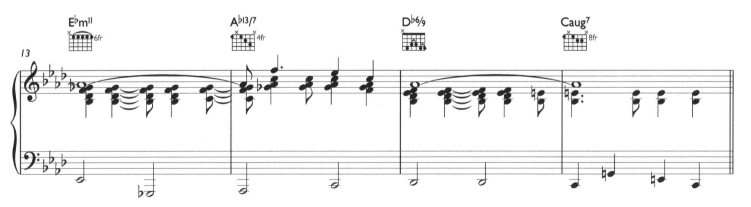

Let's Face the Music and Dance - 5 - 1

Let's Face the Music and Dance - 5 - 3

Let's Face the Music and Dance - 5 - 5

ALL OR NOTHING AT ALL

Words by
JACK LAWRENCE

Music by
ARTHUR ALTMAN

All____ or__ no - thing at all, half a love nev-er ap - pealed

____ to__ me. If your heart nev - er could yield_____ to____

All or Nothing at All - 8 - 1

me, then I'd rath-er have__ no-thing at all._____

All_____ or no-thing at all,

if it's love there___ ain't___ no in - be - ween.

Why be - gin and cry___ for some-thing that might have been,__

no___ I'd___ rath-er___ have no - thing at all.___ Please___

— don't_ put your lips so___ close to_____ my cheek, don't

smile or I'll be lost be-yond re - call.___ The kiss

in your eyes,_ the touch of your hand_ makes me_____ weak, and____ my___ heart,_

_it may grow diz - zy and fall._____

_ And if I fell un - der the spell of your call,___ I_

_ would be caught in the un - der - tow._____

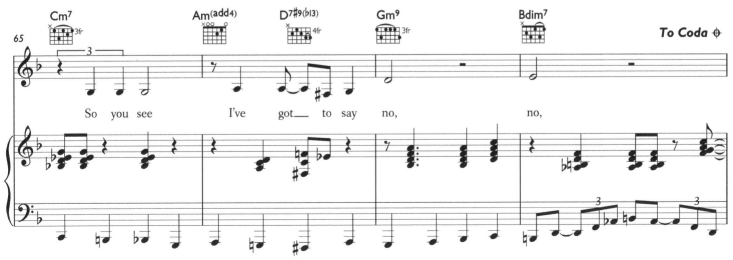

To Coda

So you see I've got__ to say no, no,

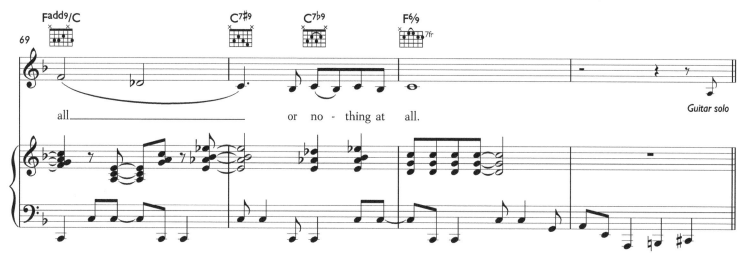

all _____ or no - thing at all.

Guitar solo

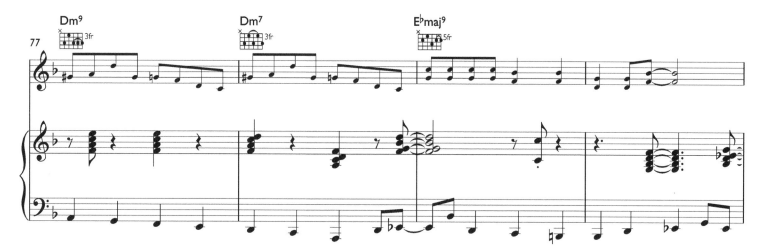

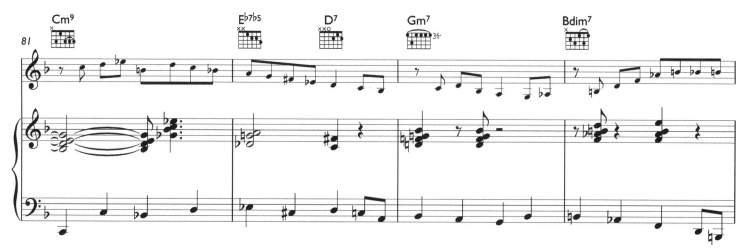

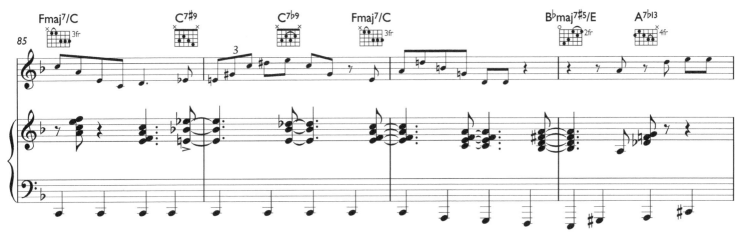

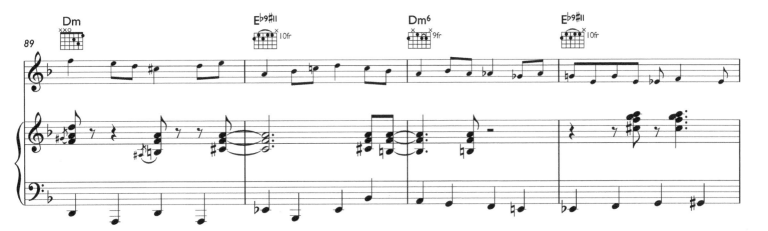

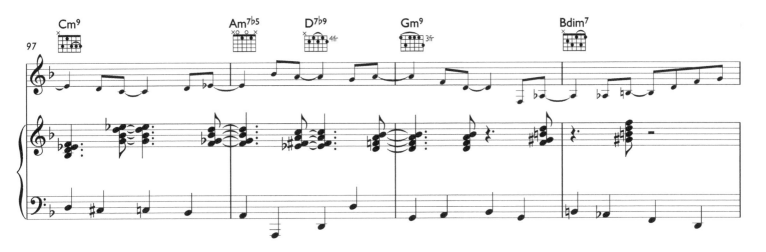

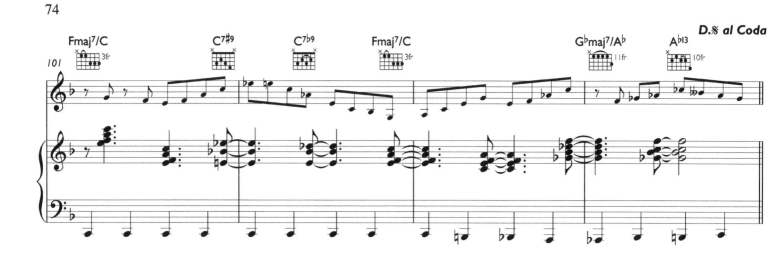

Coda

all _____ or no-thing at all.

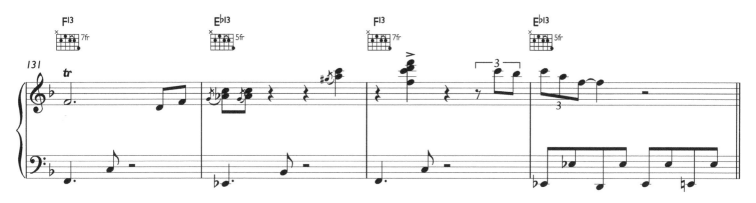

repeat ad lib. to fade

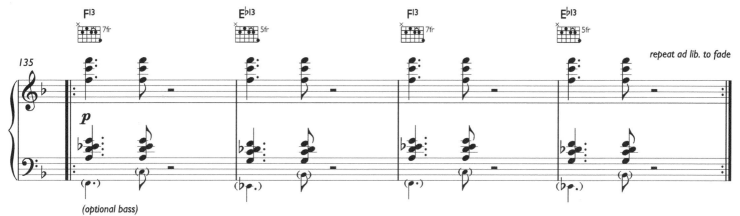

(optional bass)

ONLY THE LONELY

Words by
SAMMY CAHN

Music by
JAMES VAN HEUSEN

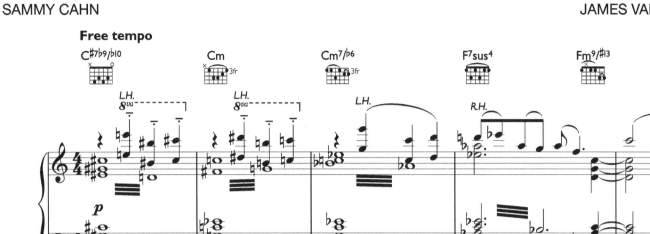

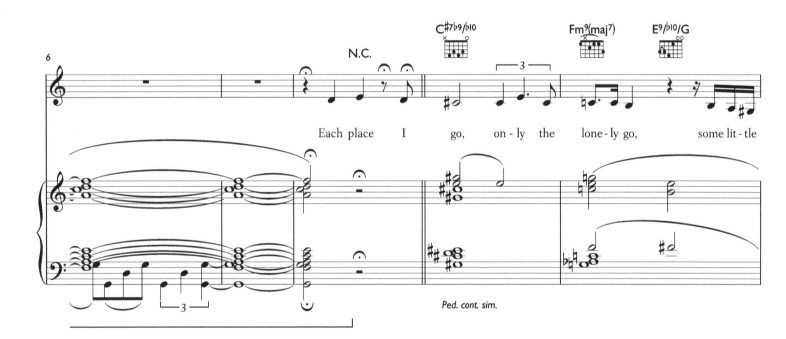

Each place I go, on-ly the lone-ly go, some lit-tle

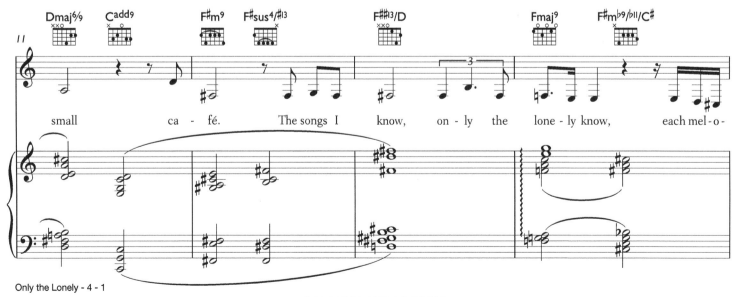

small ca-fé. The songs I know, on-ly the lone-ly know, each mel-o-

Only the Lonely - 4 - 1

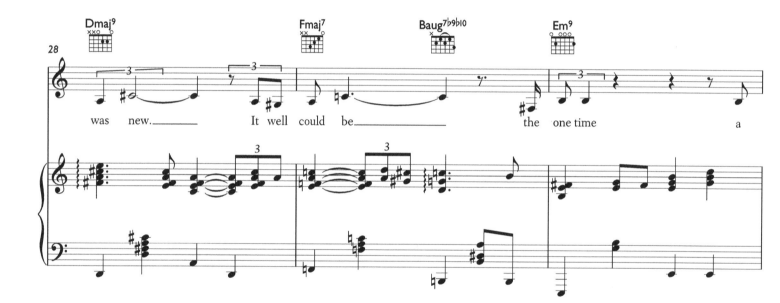

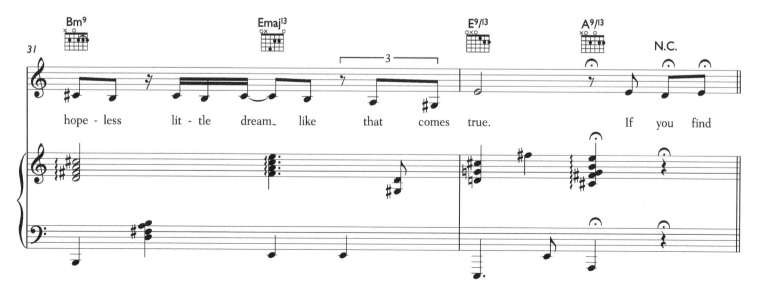

(LOOKING FOR) THE HEART
OF SATURDAY NIGHT

Words and Music by
TOM WAITS

(Looking for) The Heart of Saturday Night - 6 - 1

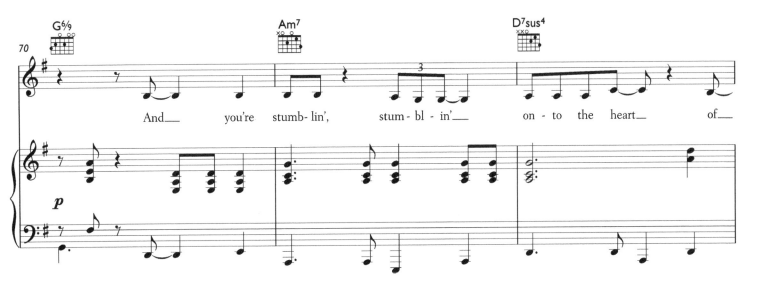

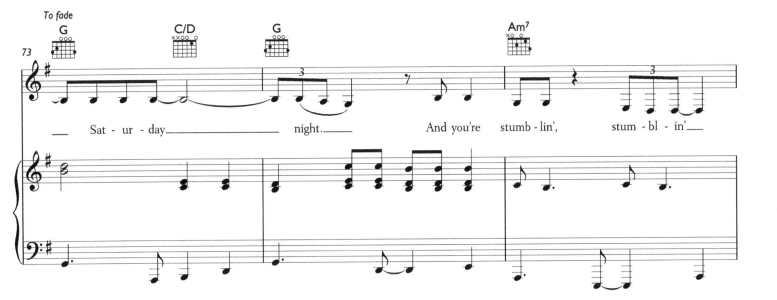

(Looking for) The Heart of Saturday Night - 6 - 6

FLY ME TO THE MOON
(IN OTHER WORDS)

Words and Music by
BART HOWARD

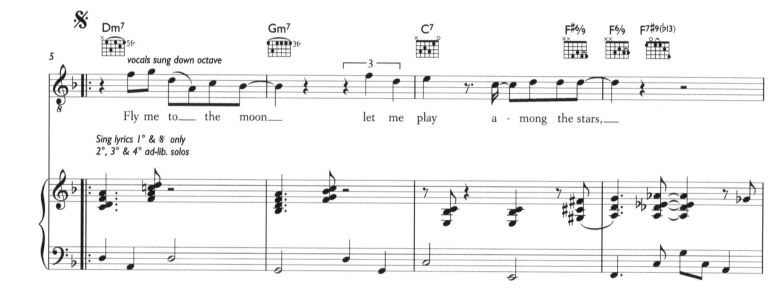

Fly me to__ the moon__ let me play a-mong the stars,__

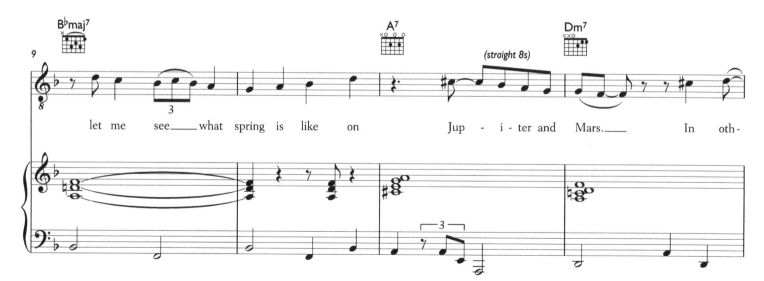

let me see__ what spring is like on Jup - i - ter and Mars.__ In oth-

Fly Me to the Moon (In Other Words) - 4 - 1

er___ words hold my hand,

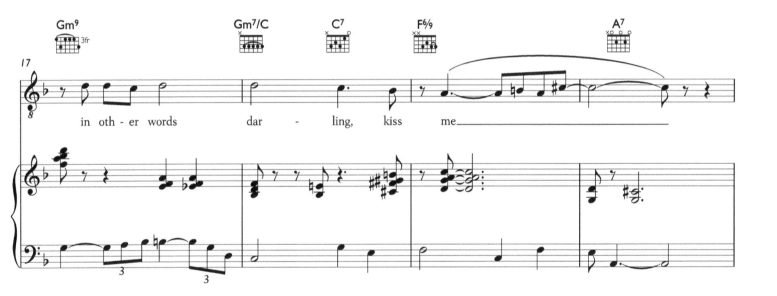

in oth - er words dar - ling, kiss me___

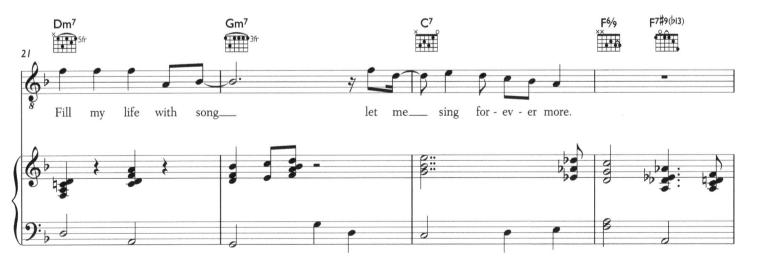

Fill my life with song___ let me__ sing for - ev - er more.

Fly Me to the Moon (In Other Words) - 4 - 2

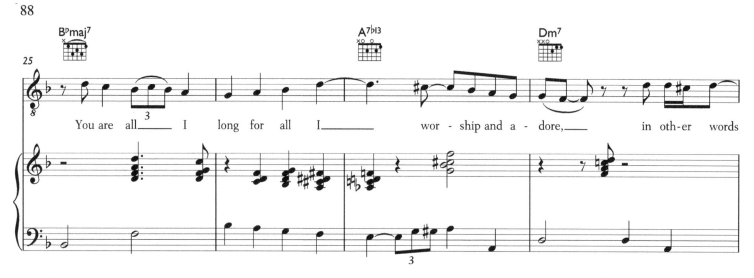

You are all___ I long for all I___ wor-ship and a-dore,___ in oth-er words

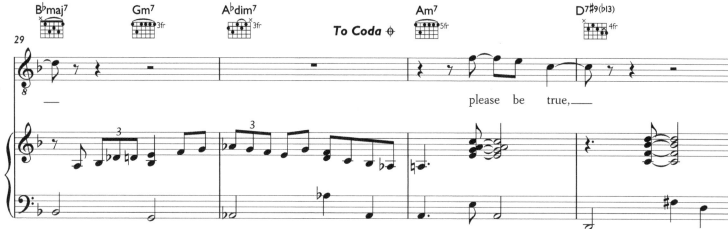

___ please be true,___

To Coda ⊕

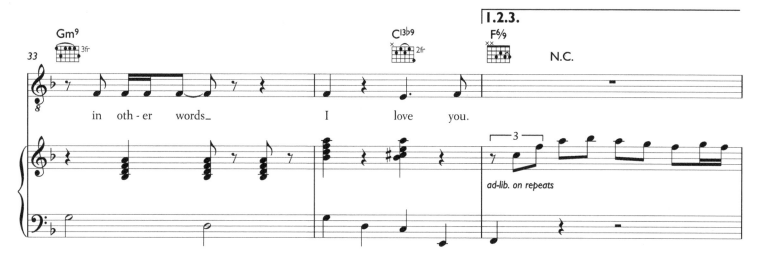

in oth-er words___ I love you.

ad-lib. on repeats

Fly_____

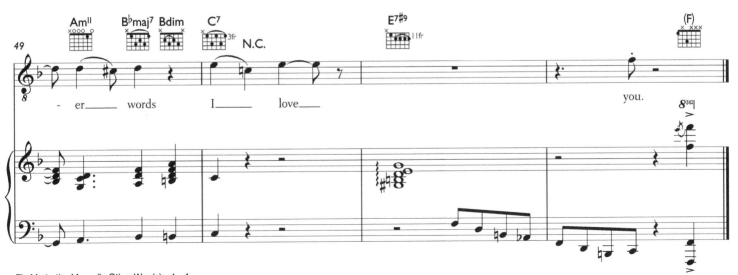

Fly Me to the Moon (In Other Words) - 4 - 4

LITTLE GIRL BLUE

Words by
LORENZ HART

Music by
RICHARD RODGERS

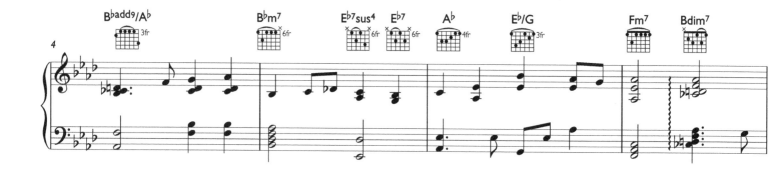

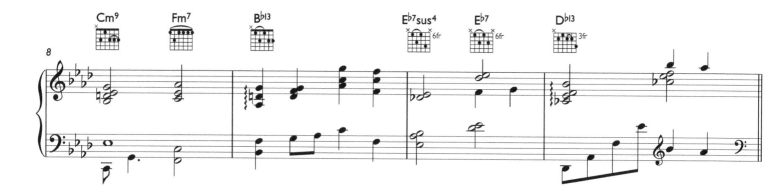

Sit there___ and count your fin - gers. What can___ you

Little Girl Blue - 7 - 1

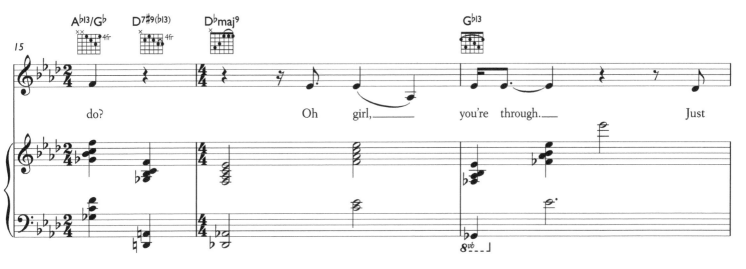

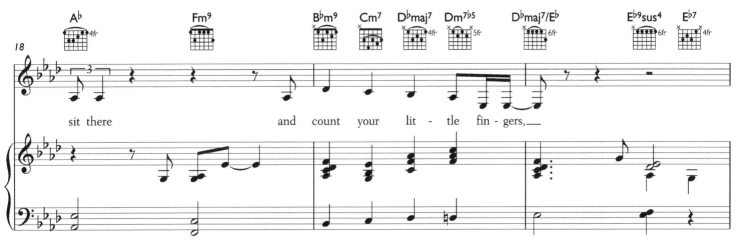

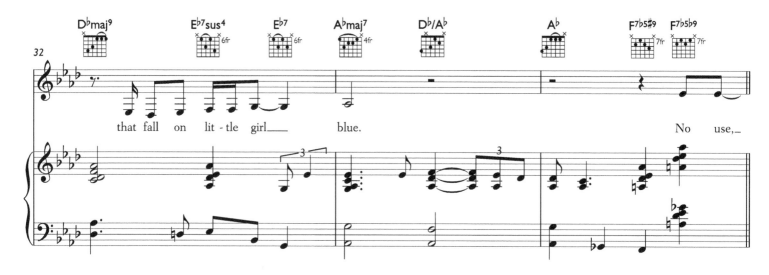

Little Girl Blue - 7 - 3

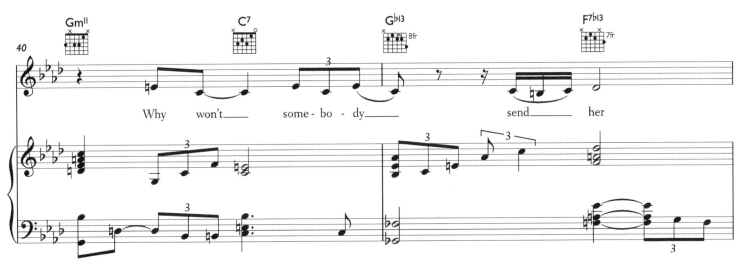

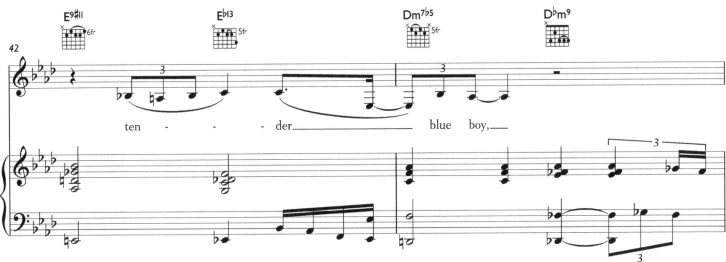

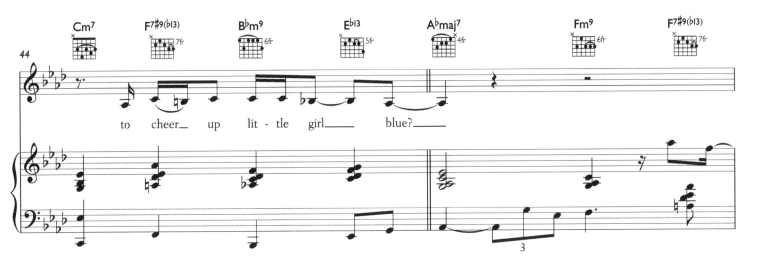

94

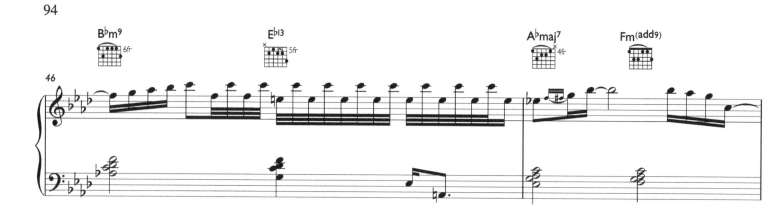

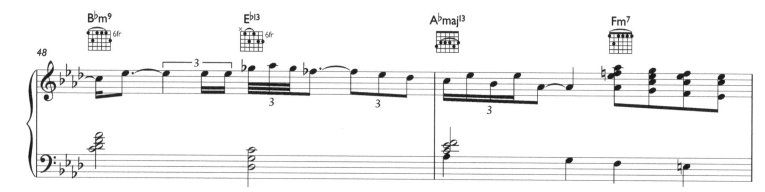

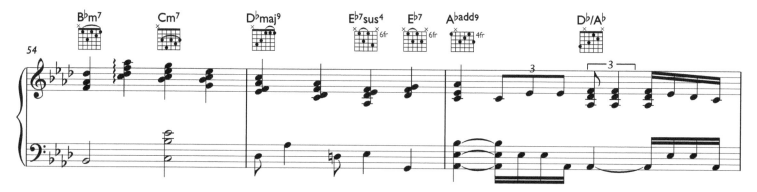

Little Girl Blue - 7 - 5

blue boy,_____ to cheer_ up lit - tle girl_____

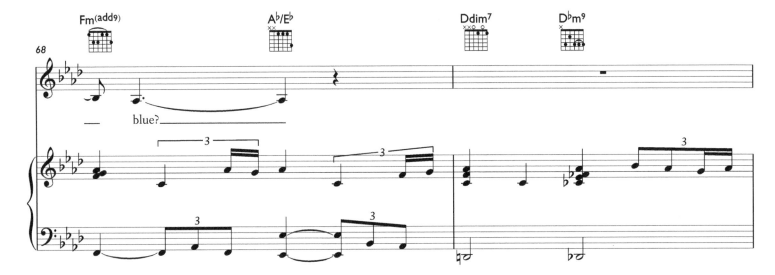

_ blue?_____

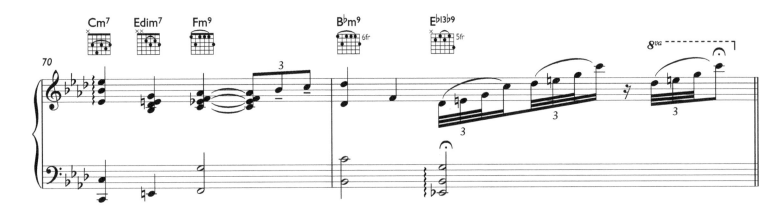

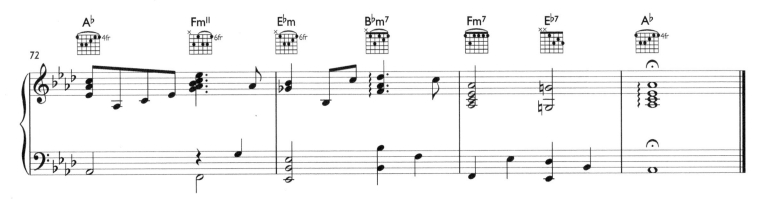